Epiphany of Light

EPIPHANY OF LIGHT

Poems and Prayers for Every Day

BY Luisella Traversi Guerra

EDITED BY
Margaret Louise Fitzgibbon

FOREWORD BY
Lucia Razza

AFTERWORD BY
Alessio Romano

RESOURCE *Publications* · Eugene, Oregon

EPIPHANY OF LIGHT
Poems and Prayers for Every Day

Resource Publications
An Imprint of Wipf and Stock Publishers
199 W. 8th Ave., Suite 3
Eugene, OR 97401

www.wipfandstock.com

PAPERBACK ISBN: 979-8-3852-6419-3
HARDCOVER ISBN: 979-8-3852-6420-9
EBOOK ISBN: 979-8-3852-6421-6

VERSION NUMBER 12/16/25

I dedicate Epiphany of Light to our new Pope Leo XIV, bearer of a wholesome American culture that I had the joy of experiencing, and as a horizon towards which I can once more direct my faith and hope.

With all my heart, I offer the third movement, Verses for America, as a posthumous remembrance to Father Peter of Boys Town in Omaha, Nebraska, to whom I owe the honor of having comprehended and shared the true meaning of 'Humanity'.

Luisella Traversi Guerra

CONTENTS

Epiphany of Light is collection of poetry and prayers for every day, presented in four movements.

Movement 2 Innermost Petals

(poems 21 to 40)

Movement 3 Verses for America

(poems 41 to 65)

Movement 4 Prayers
(poems 66 to 85)

FOREWORD

Nowadays few writers even attempt poetic composition, despite modern poetry being a more accessible art form, free from rigid metrical schemes, linguistic rules, and the use and abuse of elevated terms outdated to the point of being archaic or incomprehensible. Reading *Epiphany of Light* has given me a clear understanding of what is needed to create poetry that transforms its reader, and that is the rare talent of musicality and harmony, in honest words that speak straight to the heart.

Harmony is felt in verses where the objective description and precise details of an object, a landscape, or a person serve as a communicative bridge to abstract thoughts, emotions, experiences, and memories, ultimately opening the reader's eyes to a vision of the world beyond space and time. The true poet knows how to interpret the meaning of life and convey it - just as Luisella Traversi Guerra transmits to us her ancestral message and lifts us toward the heavens with her simple phrases such as *My heart longs for stars.*

This is a collection of four movements; *Drops of Insight, Innermost Petals, Verses for America* and *Prayers.* For me, as a Christian, it was particularly fascinating to attune myself with the poet and discover how her years living in Indiana had inspired intense poetic impressions and awakened a profound desire for artistic expression as she immersed herself in a lifestyle strikingly attractive for its precocious modernity. Indeed, it is newness, and the discovery of unknown places, that so often sparks curiosity and the urge to explore, observe, and learn: the landscapes, climate, and enchanting blooms of Indiana, the Fall foliage in Evansville, the first Christmas—these are natural, outward signs of a human need for change and evolution. It is with the arrival of the new that differences become clear when compared to what one has previously seen and experienced.

Yet there is something more that a poet like Luisella can convey to us through her poetic description: the beauty of creation and of human existence. Those who wish to accept her invitation to share her gaze can go beyond the surface, diving into the wonder of these verses filled with positivity, comfort and soul nourishment. In *"To Federica,"* the poet guides us toward an understanding of karuna—a Sanskrit term meaning the active desire to relieve the suffering of others, implying care and attention toward one's neighbor, especially those enduring hardship and illness, and their carers and loved ones who so often suffer in silence. Harmony manifests when a perfect alchemy and balance are achieved between the concrete and the abstract, between word and meaning. In every nuance, the wonder of a minute detail and its uniqueness are exalted in Luisella's poetry. It does not lack reflections on the complex reality of human existence, including its less joyful aspects. In *"Doubt"* one senses the anxiety of modern man and the decline of absolute moral values such as brotherhood and respect. Centuries-old prejudices have been overcome, yet we have been overwhelmed and chained by virtual illusions, through our constant photographing and posting, and by material illusions, such as limiting ourselves to satisfying the need to possess goods, even useless and superfluous ones.

We must find a way to evolve before we grow fully numb what is essential within us: willpower, sensitivity, care, and patience - qualities that distinguish us, which we are passively surrendering, along with the cultivation of good feelings, spirituality, and the drive to love authentically. This collection serves to counteract these negative tendencies. Luisella's poetic thought is founded on love, and her journey ultimately leads to faith in God, the beginning and end of all things, and of human existence itself. Earthly harmony rises to eternal harmony, to a God who saves humanity from evil both outside and in, who illuminates the darkness when hearts are weak or lost, and guides us to seek refuge and relief from suffering in our faith. As in ancient times, human beings naturally yearn for an instinctive connection with the Universe, for life beyond death. *Epiphany of Light* resonates with this deepest feeling, where the poet's verses express the highest spirituality, revealed in religious contemplation, in Christianity.

In the final movement, *Prayers*, she infuses us with her certainty of a generous God who will save our souls and reunite them with Him through His infinite power of Love, prevailing over everything, in spite of everything, always.

Lucia Razza
Cultural Curator
October 6, 2025

DROPS OF INSIGHT

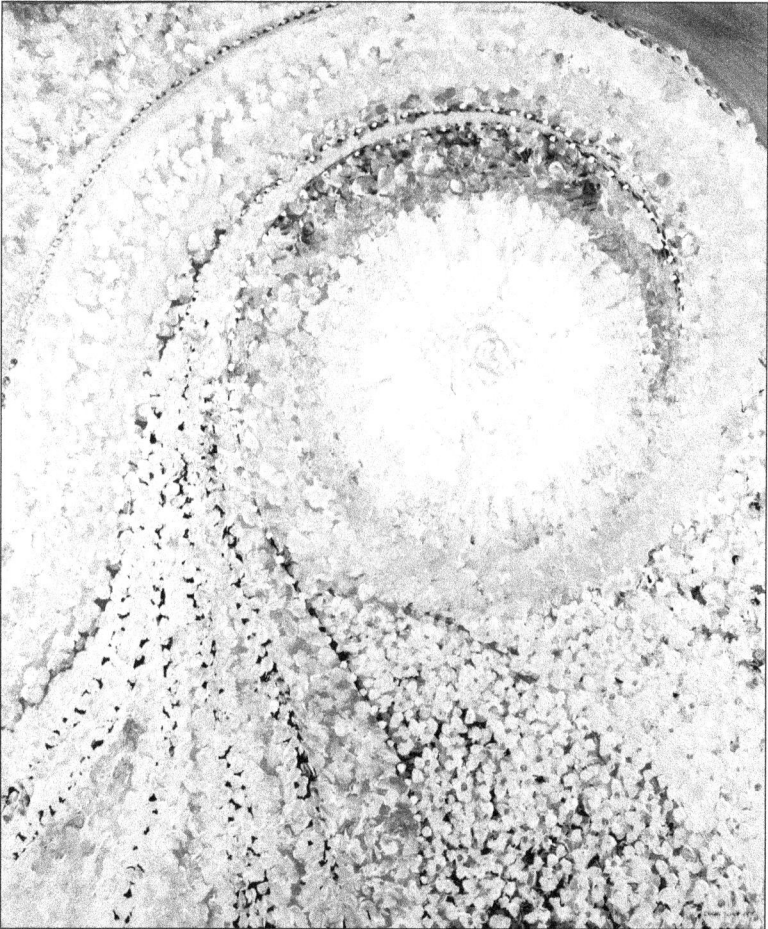

01 POETRY PIECE

Poetry . . .
strange song,
free,
light,
inexplicable,
unforeseeable.
Breath,
heart music!

02 IN SEARCH OF STARS

Desperately, in search of stars
I walk down the path
of my destiny.
Deep is the breath
waiting to find
the isolation and acceptance of my present day.
Like an archer armed,
I bend the bow,
I shoot the arrow,
and my heart takes fire.

03 DOUBT

Beaten against the rocks
of doubt and distress,
my soul wavers between two dimensions,
the possible and the impossible.

A noise, a pain,
a knocking at my mind.
The need to overcome
the infinite want of a mother
—to satisfy justice and equality
and chase after true love.

What should I do? What should I not?
How to lovingly support the educative process
on meeting my children now adults?
Give, give, give.

Giving to one and to the other
in equal measure,
how far apart are the needs of each?
What good is equality
if each life is different?
If one of them suffered
from a greater pain,
if his dream was shattered,
opening onto a bitterer path,
how to give lovingly?

Patience, expectation, measure,
a welcome so dear to my heart,
leading to the carefully weighed act.
Yet at odds with doubt and torment
the heart grasps.
What is it right to do?

04 COMING BACK TO FIGHT

I left you in silence
my poet and friend,
and I did not care for you
any longer.

Speak to me now
while I hear this cry
rising within
and invoking him.

Though tired, the hero
has put his helmet on
and again gone down
to the arena, among
the wild and growling beasts.

You alone, my hero
will win for love.
They will not succeed in
destroying the fortress!

The solid defences stand,
and inside
rebirth
waits for peace.

05 THE EMPTY SPACE

Vacuum,
inward space,
abyss of mystery and torment.

A new way shakes
the solid-built rhythm.

and prepares . . .
In which future
will the present break out?

New perceptions and knowledge
challenge the now anchored
enthusiasm, tastes, and convictions.

Dreams in vain,
achievements lost,
and nothing is worthy bright.

Only immense emptiness
calls forth to decry
this knawing of new and true life.

06 OFFSPRING OF MYSTERY

We have been summoned by the Mystery
from unknown places,
thanks to an act of Love,
passing through woman's body,
we came.

Born upside-down,
the path unknown
decoded day by day,
deemed to love and change
giving Life meaning.

The place found,
opening our eyes
with dismayed breath,
astonished and frightened.
Act one: weeping.

Heaven, work, food,
but beyond the relief
of love
and mother's milk,
the void is Paradise.

Suddenly
a short trail
cuts its way to measure,
trials and woes
loosening the sense

of being children of another world.
We could just say
that we are desperate,
confused, cheated,
that horror comes from the pain
of being living creatures.

But . . .

We are offspring of a Mystery
overflowing with Love.

It speaks to our heart
of Life beyond,
to be reached,
discovering in our actions
our guiding messages.

Living each moment
tied to the golden thread
knotting our destinies,
we receive and we give,
and the journey to heaven begins.

We, kin, bred of a Mystery,
only in Love
conquer the vision,
the meaning and the value of Life.

07 NOSTALGIA FOR A FADED DREAM

Nostalgia for a faded dream
that time had awarded us
but then took back again,
so life's wounds reopen.

Pulsing wounds beat out the adventure,
Exhausting, while loving you, measuring
with growth, enrooting you in a place
from where you will be ripped out.

An echo of us dreamt
somewhere on earth,
belonging to the soul, alone,
an echo resounding within us,
sky-blue enchantment.

Feelings coddled and laid bare,
identity in perfect harmony
between wishes and true life,
solid, silent, pondered
and savoured day by day.

Moments gushing out from the heart,
a gaping hole within
while opening to the new.
Even the mother tongue
is a barrier in that village,

Where all men are brothers along the way
but do not understand your actions,
where growing means hunger for adventure
and a new civilization often melds with misfortune.

Nostalgia is riding the world,
a suffocating emotion,
because everything exists
but nothing lasts—forever.

08 A SHOT

My weakness
like a ball rebounds,
launched afar it
comes right back
to the hand
that threw it.

I want to crush it,
seize it on the rebound
—desire to distance
myself mirror strong—
both hands pick it up,
launch it high, and score,
centring the basket.

Joyful but unceasing
until I do stop—
the game won,
my weakness will disappear.

Don't dribble away,
just play offense.

09 SEPTEMBER

A subtle uneasiness
of torpor or of weakness
drags my heart,
while in my thoughts
a sibilating tangle
taps and beats.

My inner tension
wrestles with my sinner self.
Repressing, denying,
breaking out from within,
like a stifled cry,
wishing to explode.

Ups and downs in my life:
perpetual dualism between
responsibility and imagination,
consciousness or dream,
solidity or carelessness,
loyalty to everyday toil or freedom?

Hamlet's eternal question,
"to be or not to be?",
shadow of fear
of discordance,
of any break in our life,
so neat, tidy, loyal.

But way beyond this life
does that frontier land exist
where the yearning
for everyday chores comes true,
with my mind in the future
and my heart among the stars?

10 WINTER PICTURE

In the garden among cold branches,
you are hopping in search of a seed
or a crumb of bread.

In the grass between the gray and the dark green
your red plumage catches my eye,
and restores something joyful and merry.
Oh my robin-redbreast!

The branches flung to the sky
sparkle in the light,
illuminating trunk-knots,
drawing dreamt up sculptures.

Up above pearly clouds, roaming
like my thoughts, are swirling
around the center of a felt
yearning and silence.

Now, exactly as it did many years ago,
a robin is hopping in the garden,
where my laughing sons
ran and chased each other.

Far-off days, but still carved on my heart,
bygone times, yet alive,
notes of a life incised
by warm love signs.

Winter is now upon us,
in its soundless silence dressed,
making way for the new,
pressing its advance.
Oh robin, friend of this ancient rite,
bring here once more
the steady beat of life.

Origin of everything—
thought, action or unfurling leaf,
everything starts again,
everlasting, everything, a glorious opportunity.

11 THE FAINT HOPE

Hope is like a subtle thread—
the web a little spider
weaves on human destiny, hung
as sentinel above doors
herald of strength and valor.

When a wave of sadness
or a sharp pain
might stifle us,
it suddenly resurges
as our shield and parapet.

Then, in mute perseverance
from fertile fonts,
life, imagination, and poetry
bubble with new energy,
all transfused with hope.

12 I CHING MULTIPLE MOVING LINES

I consulted the I Ching
and it pointed out to me:
'Small dominating force'.

Rabbit:
moral strength
gentle behaviour.

The suggestion:
infinite patience
no dignity lost.

What a message!

13 IF

Were the light within me,
if truth would guide my way . . .
but nothing gushes out
in this moment.

The poet is silent.
The mind triumphs.

14 FEBRUARY MORNING

Look at the enchantment
of the sun splitting
the rainy gray of winter
inside a pink cloud.
How serene my heart is!
Have a good day, life!

15 FINDING PLACE WITHIN SELF

Let me find again a place in my soul
where I can locate love once more,
where I can rest little and listen
to the rounded echo rising from the drops of music
falling into the clear water of an underground spring.

Plink!
and the echo amplifies an arcane emotion,
an excitement summons your human courage
and tells you what is worthwhile and what is not,
and again proposes a fitting choice
a well-shod pair of shoes to quicken your steps.

Light conditions,
a feeling of balance,
sensations of peace, fairness toward yourself and others,
strength enough to succeed in doing
that duty that has been ours for time immemorial
but, fearful, for we did not desire change.

Behold, there the field of rotating sunflowers
chasing daylight from dawn to dusk
opening into your eyes.

Discover them beautiful and humble in their summer splendour
like feeling alive in an ocean of silent love!
Then the fruits of life become evident and beloved
and everything tastes full of summertime.

16 MUSIC AND RHYTHM

Waxing moon, western hump
Swinging clear in the misty October sky.
The bell tower pushes upwards
to the sky, while a star sparkles
at the first sunset of joy.
The bell rings to welcome the night,
covering the hearts of those who hope and pray.

In the silent emptiness the sound is distilled
of the now yellowed leaf
rocking on the wings of the wind.
A listlessness pierces through me
and this weightiness of old and moldy queries
engages me in giving rest
to the discouraged soul.

Time passes by and fast unrolls
those days, as years alike,
into the uproar
of a single instant.
Time coagulating, clots of life
born in pain but hiding that seed of joy.
yet to be discovered.

Which secret to reveal
and nightmare of relativity to dissolve?
Behold now all the stars sparkling,
prayers arise from the heart and breath
of life's rhythm.

It is customary
to flood the soul with notes
of divine music.

17 THE KITE

Flying in the fresh April wind
the kite of my life,
light, among worn memories,
buried in the wounded heart.

Free, it carries me high
looking down serene and quiet
on the distance covered
in the inmost, mine deep in me.

The unburied treasure
releases a trail of well-being
flooded with joy
and exploding.

How long the journey of life,
trying to cleanse the past,
lost in wrinkles of feelings
—a child prisoner

to the emptiness of a denied kiss
or a never heard wish.

Now the way is neat and ordered,
the glance is clear, bright,
now the heart flies free in the blue light
because the meaning is revealed.

18 HEART AND LIFE

Suspended in the instant
contemplating,
appears the image
of a heart.
Adorned with
pearls and diamonds,
it circles above
light and precious,
illuminating my life.

Mysteriously,
feelings and thoughts,
dancing drops,
memories appear,
yearning sighs,
sweet nothings
intertwined
silently
in empty space.

19 SHIFT OF WIND

The wind is shifting
and humanity is plotting its new course.

It rocks
the footsteps of the previous path,
while the meaning becomes
stronger and clearer
for those who want responsibility and love.

This wind brings trust and courage,
patience and humility,
tenure and serenity,
dreams and artistry.

20 CHRISTMAS IS COMING

Heavy days,
pantingly anticipating
a slice of sky, where one can breathe.

Dancing anxieties,
whirling through the mind
like leaves in the wind.

Mood and perceptions
in contrast with faith,
which believe neither in the instant
nor in relativity.

Eyes lowered, closed,
counting the shuffling steps
of this inexplicable
ponderous gait.

Everything appears and disappears
chasing in shadows, in light,
. . . when at last
through a dull mesh I perceive

a glimpse of color where
new, transformed,
I find myself again, now . . .
Christmas is coming!

'Catharsis from the old
to the new being'

Burnt by the world's uproar,
very gentle, impalpable
the soul hovers
and sails clear.

MOVEMENT 2

INNERMOST PETALS

21 WINTER MORNING

The sky drips
into the grey fog,
the streetlamp frays
its weak light,
a strong scent of wet leaves
floods the dark
of the winter morning.

The town is still sleeping,
but here and there a window twinkles.
The eyes peeping out
wander far and now,
in the kitchen, coffee is bubbling
and its flavour embracing
all the house.

Little gestures and actions
accompanying us
day by day,
building the way
of the country life,
as in the memories
of my childhood.

22 FEBRUARY IS HERE

Damp color
fades into pearl-grey
frost; it is February!

Hungry for buds,
for the blackbird song
solemnly announcing: it is February!

A lovely, light bird
robin red-breast
heads long and gives a hop

onto the brittle branch
and slowly, gently dangles
while the day is rising clear.

Everywhere the frost whitens,
the robin goes far away,
in the cold the ice sparkles.

How I do love February!
This month gives signs I welcome
like lessons of life and calling.

The moment is hard,
but promises a better tomorrow.
The pruned branch points to the future.

So, a strict teacher is he
who recreates, from the void,
the flame to forge with wisdom,
but not without pain,
from the heart's core a push
to advance and improve more.

23 IMAGES FROM THE FUTURE

Images from the future
swirling within me
not yet disclosed
to an attentive ear.

Everything is on the edge!
Into the abyss, or take flight
towards a new tomorrow
yet to be generated.

Life!
Embracing Mystery
you reveal yourself
only when tomorrow has come.

I open my arms
and even if toiling
I wait:
to weep or to exalt?

24 SICK TOWN

Noises,
din in the air
sink down
into our dry soul.

Distant shouts,
far away
alone
sick is the town.

25 DROP OF LIFE

Sweet
the drop of life
trembling in
the new thought.

Fresh
the blooming vitality
rising and
the deed is young.

26 DANCING SHAPES

Shaded, soft, fast,
in the heart
appear
gentle dancing shapes,
made of light.

Sailing gently,
sliding within
but then disappear
as soon as the mind
wants to imprison them.

They open and free
notes of art, love
beauty,
lending rhythm to one's breath
and transforming reality.

An explosion of colors
floods over me seeking
the dark side of pain,
the enthusiastic stream of joy,
the birth of love.
I welcome them: life's teachers!

27 WORDS

Words sparkling with love
deep, in the heart's cavern,
syllabizing experience,
passing with its veil
of love and joy
which flowing sweeps all away,
brimming and clarifying
the days of life,
the days of growth.

Words born of love,
powerful energy transforming
sour into sweet
abuse into justice,
intemperance into rules,
vulgarity into style,
isolation into embrace,
roughness into tenderness,
scratch into caress,
misunderstanding into dialogue,
want into unity,
desperation into belief,
nothingness into light,
ugliness into beauty,
solitude into Prayer.

28 HAVING CONFIDENCE

As the flower of the April bloom bends
down in the foam of moist air,
trusting the coming season.

As the nest chirping merrily,
while buds and violets open all around,

As the child running in the park, jumps
happy for his moment of time,

As the woman flinging open her house
makes it clean and shine again,

As the man setting about his work
which yields his dignity and bread

As the old man walks quiet
on the road leading him far away

So my heart opens on tomorrow
confident that the New going forth
is the path which builds a patch of life again;
it watches and waits for its action time
for the final step
born from the original design

of two young spouses,
faithful foundation honoring reality.
Driven by a dream
which respects the value of work
as space in human growth.

29 MY BELOVED LITTLE EARTH

My little Earth
navigating
in an infinite universe of stars,
I carry you in my heart.
My wonderful Earth
special in the Galaxy,
casket of light,
you, all dressed in white and blue!
Generous mother who feeds
the invisible insect and the mammoth elephant,
you, fertile, generous, tireless,
in your innards sprout
plants, flowers of every species and beauty.
You, creator of extraordinary scenarios!
Thank you, for your divine gift,
patrimony of wisdom and knowledge,
inspirer and medic of life anew.
My incredible little Earth, thank you!
Humanity now once again crazed
in a devouring Anthropocene,
transformer of change
that manifests itself in the form of pain
that plagues the future with brutality and fear.
Dominions of cruel powers,
famished by infernal yearnings,
void of knowledge,
blind to Infinity.
My beloved earth,
forgive us!

30 MY HEART SAILS

My heart sails lightly
on fields,
of grain,
of life.

My glance is sweeping.
Serene,
on the golden wheat
of Love I feel
vibrating in me.

The seed harvested in June,
the caretaker of the new,
planted in the earth,
will become tomorrow.

Still the old snakes—
but fire and light cleanse anew
and the fresh furrow
can emerge at last.

Between misty yesterday and clear tomorrow
the forces of Good divide.

31 PLACES IN THE WORLD

There are places
belonging
only to the soul
always flickering within.

A green meadow surrounded by
high poplar rows, sun bright.
Hills soft planted
with sweet smelling vines
golden and ripe, to reap fields of grain.

Proud villages
their ancient belltowers, and houses
leaning against each other
holding each other up.
Rivers and streams, gurgling water
down distant immaculate mountains.

And the sea of everything,
great reverser, force generator, color maker.
And still towns, thousands of towns,
of their history haughty,
of their past proud,
of their beauty spoiled.

But there are places
lying deep in our souls,
between dreams and poetry,
enchantment and fantasy

Oases of love and serenity,
where we discover
our true world
is there at last, and forever.

32 MY GARDEN

My garden is
the heart place
where all my troubles
seep away at last.

The scattered colors and rhythms
evoke in me
a walk, in a process, to be conquered,
only by the advancement of conscious life.

Anxiety lands
on the fresh and new green
of the just sown meadow
in the shadow of the age-old pine tree.

The palms shivering
with the breeze,
a reminder of something exotic
far from daily life.

The olive tree
with its silver leaves
promises a lifetime long,
the flowers on the limes
intense scents exhale beyond.

Here and there colorful bushes
and flowers, flowers for every season
but the sweet queen lavender,
spreads lively like an echo of the sea.

Peeping out of the balconies
the vermillion and generous geranium,
and the hanging wisteria in clusters,
embellish that quiet corner to ponder.

While mounting the great staircase,
in ecstasy I listen
to the mystery of the bright jasmine
flooding everywhere.

My garden is a corner
the place where all life's troubles
of a workday are quietened
and my heart rests.

33 SILENCE IN MY HOME

This silence in the most tidy
and quiet home
is the peace of my mind and my hope
that a better future
is heading at us.

In this precious hour
of ecstatic serenity
it is revealed to me
the deep and true sense
of what we are living.

I am Christian,
no advantages nor favours
to lead my life,
my only talisman
the way I am taking.

It is a saving thread
which keeps one from falling
into the inevitably illusory
drama of facts,
unchaining us to the relativity
of the moment being.

In the spirit of Christ
an implicit latch
allowing the disclosure of a light
which does not belong to us
but is made of us,
steering us clear.

34 THE LAUREL TREE

Under the dirty ruins
in a yard crumbling down
a small, modest laurel
is fighting to survive
ugliness all around.

Things ageless and shapeless
piling up, the ground cracks
and the foundations of a new wall rise
among hovels chilled by centuries of want.

Old structures lasting for years
to defend humble and hard-working people
without hopes nor desires.
Poverty crowned with laurels
misery and poetry,
history celebrated by the strength
of a blessed and stubborn tree.

"You honored the world
in the long run untouched
and for years you observe
that simple life
without art, or beauty,
or any desire to change"

And now that time demolished
the old walls of a
stinking and dusty stable
torn open to the sky
unveiling
the laurel tree.

"You are small, clumsy but beautiful reminding us again
that Mother Earth, patient and generous,
even in the most sordid places,
buds and with lovingness transforms".

35 PLACES SPEAK TO ME

Places speak to me
of shapes and colors,
of light and shadow,
of feelings and emotions.

I discover in myself
the artist's impetus
and everything in that action is joy!

36 HUSBAND AND WIFE

Sweet is the path
chosen in our dream

firm is the path
we begin hand in hand

a great love binds
and wraps us together,

a sweet glance
entwines our lives.

Today we are married,
pioneers of the future,

abandoned in His arms
and committed to the Mystery

and blossoming in the joy
of the future to come.

37 LIFE AS A MUSICAL SCORE

Beautiful is
the blank sheet of paper
with the lines well
drawn and aligned.
In them I perceive
the thread of a score
that orchestrates the music
of my life.

38 TO THE GREAT POPE WOJTYLA

Behold now he walks
among ears of wheat
floating in the sun
hand in hand
with golden angels.

A scent of lilies
spread through the air,
white clouds
and songs of glory,
and music is joy.

Behold, now strength
has returned as before
and man is the holy image
of love, work,
and coherence.

His life is a gift for everyone,
His work is the master road,
His story honors history.
He is a great one and forever will be,
the Great Pope Wojtyla
within our souls forever lives.

39 SPECIAL NIGHT

The town seems astonished
by silence soaking it.
A thick and gloomy fog
blankets all over.

The streets are deserted
but in windowsills
a certain "something"
of peace resounds.

Each window twinkles
with flickering lights
and a scent of holiday
shines through.

A time for home life,
a time for family,
a time for unity,
it is Christmas time.

40 AMONGST THE ANCESTORS

My ancestors' graves are a place
I feel summoned to.
To persevere in my search
for tomorrow—
for a witness,
for justice and good,
love and dignity,
guidance and respect.

How much I desire
to be a flash of light
in the present of my life!
To rest at last
and not be afraid
of having sowed
evil, untruth, weakness,
without having to ask
anybody to forget.

I want to live
in nobility and dignity so
I do aspire to good!

VERSES FOR AMERICA

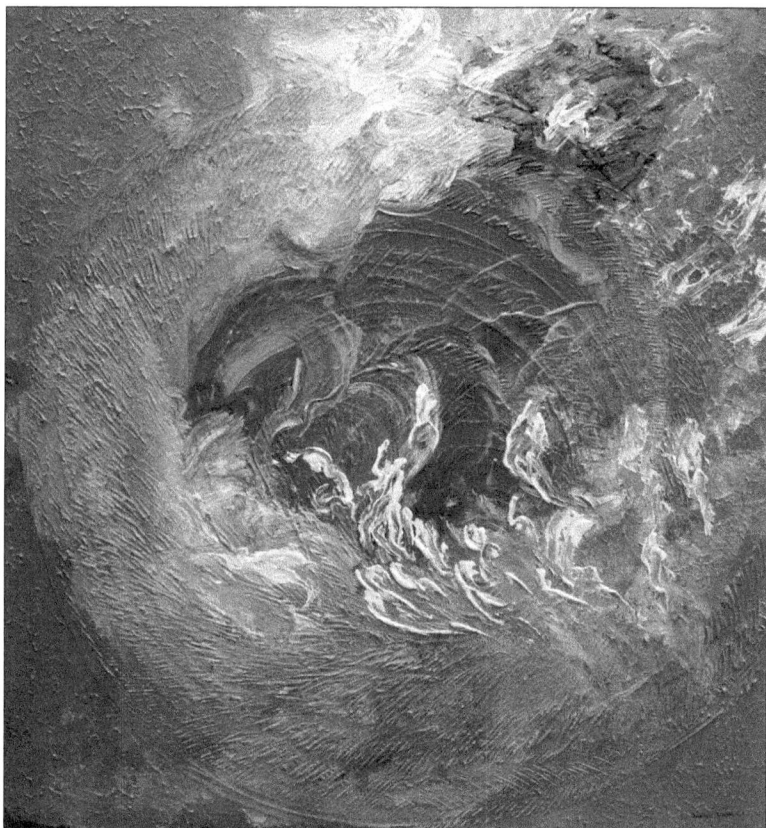

41 DIARY

Outside, the sun shines
in Oak Meadow,
where time seeps in
like another reality.

Harmony hovers, and
the background music
makes the afternoon
languid and a little romantic.

I'm waiting for you,
muse of dreams,
path of fantasy,
sweet artistic soul.

How I love that flow
from deep within:
a shape, a color,
a sweet feeling.

Opening up and discovering,
with amazement, seeing oneself
accepted by the "child"
who sings life.

I attempt the adventure
—it opens like a
gift, but I look at it
with fear.

A few
moments
more . . . .
. . . and everything will be done.

42 THE WHOLE EARTH

The sky is so clear
and the air so bright
that, pointedly,
a feeling troubles me;
the impossibility
of communicating it,
And the fear of making it
banal.

The rosy sunset
of the evening seems
now a purplish cloak
spread over the earth.

America,
a land still fresh,
unburdened
by the past lives
of old men.

America still rich
in dreams and hopes,
you want to steal my soul
in love with an old, and trampled
Italy.

While my heart
struggles
between alternating feelings,
love grows within me
for the whole earth,
my homeland among the stars
of a mysterious firmament,
that swiftly
flows toward infinity.

43 IN INDIANA

America, America,
a land lush
as far as the eye can see.

Ancient oaks like warriors
tell stories of a distant
unreal world . . .

The silent step
of the friendly Indian
left a light footprint
like that of a fox
or a fleeing rabbit,
and now the sovereign
eagle still dominates the skies.

In the immense,
orderly greenery,
the care and love in the houses
calm the anxious toil
of those who, seeking new lands,
have encountered
this welcoming paradise.

Beautiful America,
a new world dreamed of,
made real,
made of people
who know how to innovate.

44 ON THE WINTER ROADS IN EVANSVILLE

Leaves chase each other madly,
rustling, crunching
on the gray asphalt
battered by the icy wind.

In eddies, forward, backward,
looking for a place
where they can quietly
land and transform.

So too, I feel,
in the present moment,
forward, backward, swirling
in a dancing whirlwind.

I long for a feeling
that will give me new impetus;
to try again,
to dream,
of a life,
to love.

45 STRENGTH AND POWER

Strength and power
have these spaces,
swirling with blue and white clouds.
These skies can attract like a magnet
to greater aspirations,
or crush you
with a leaden gray
mired in a
land wounded by
the civilization of the end of the century.

46 SNOW BEFORE CHRISTMAS

It falls lightly, confusedly,
in wandering grayness,
this whispering snow.
It calms you, envelops you,
tickles your face,
layering its precious crystal flakes,
impalpable and swirling.

What joy is snow!
A child's eyes
opening in a dim memory
of a somewhat harsh day
in somewhat hard times,
and the playful smile of times
gone by transforms everything.

Look, the tree dressed in white
decorates the garden,
and the magnolia leaf grows broad,
bending under the unaccustomed weight.

A streetlamp has put on
its cap, and the asphalt sports a
silken scarf.
The snow flutters dreamily,
and thoughts strike me unawares.

How we too, senselessly,
in our actions,
wander in a whirling world.

A little here, a little there
doubts waver
and the (also) impalpable hour of
a cycle—finished history
waits for a bud
of new life to blossom.
And meanwhile, time
snows, snows, snows!

47 THAW

The joyful sun
thawing
the hard, brilliant
frost on the countryside,
promises me a day both
industriously serene
and constructive.

Ah, how we are
children of this land,
how
involved
we are
in its metaphysical
Mysteries.

48 CHRISTMAS LULLABY

The choir of angels sings in the heart,
the drop of love sings in the heart,
falling into the void
and opening the doors
to Christmas.

In the whiteness
a soul smiles,
a wave of joy,
whispers,
rises;
it is a sweet
Christmas lullaby.

49 GOOD MORNING, LIFE

Good morning, life,
so demanding
and impenetrable in the
mystery that surrounds you,
but life, life, life
that lives in me.

50 WE LOOKED AT EACH OTHER SMILING

We looked at each other smiling
because together
we were discovering
the next step to take,
the next areas to improve.

We were serene . . .
We were dynamic . . .
We were humble . . .
We were growing.

51 THE SASSAFRAS

The frozen sassafras,
today, to my amazement,
has returned to quivering,
in the air warmed
by a ray of sunshine.

So too is my hope
rekindled
in opening myself to the courage
of not letting myself
irremediably bend.

I too will go back to planning
And to dreaming.

52 EASTER SKY

Upward,
toward the sky,
in a periwinkle blue
that envelops the universe
and perpetually transforms us.

Toward the star,
in the light
that orients and guides,
in the faith of a Love
that is the bread of Life.

Happy Easter!

53 IN FLIGHT

The wing
of the glistening plane
shines
in a periwinkle-colored
sky.
Dazzling light, deep emotion.

Flying,
in a dimension of myself
that seems to belong
to another
reality.

Floating
in the unbreathable air,
where everything is conquest,
where only dreams
dressed in technology
can attempt to overcome human limits.

Here I find myself
calm, serene,
in this virtual, present
Reality.

54 THE TRAIN

The train passes fast,
sending its greeting
of hope and thrust.

It passes quickly,
shaking my thoughts
lazy and sleepy
on this summer afternoon.

It passes in a flash
like youth
that, singing to itself,
soon departs.

Behold the silence
after the last echo
of a shrieking whistle
bidding farewell to the water.

So life, like ripples,
like that silence
like a thought
my train goes.

55 THE SIGN

Stretched in the sun,
the cane in the ditches
bending lightly,
caressed by that warm wind
along the road—it
flies beyond
thought.

The asphalt shimmers
and the car moves;
the feeling shimmers
light, light,
and my heart
dreams of tomorrow.

The American duck flies
alongside its companion;
the sign is positive,
and the day is saved.
Let's go!
It's time to move.

56 ENVELOPED BY THAT FIELD

Thus swimming among
golden ears of corn
in the June sun,
my soul
blessed itself
by gathering that sign
of prosperity:
wheat,
the bread of life.

Like a light, floating shape
I felt myself inside,
enveloped by that field
and in the magic
and enchantment,
I savored its abundance
to the limit
of human possibility.

57 SOLAR ECLIPSE

Children of the universe,
brothers of the stars,
lost in space,
knights of a world
to come.

Slender structures
within a system
that we dare only surmise
or believe is true.

But today the moon has
eclipsed the sun.

The remote echo that
governs us has pointed out
the mystery to us, allowing us
to touch it with our hands.
What a sense of reverence
for this half-light
at midday!

58 SILENCE

With our hearts suspended
in wonder at
what
surrounds us,
what
moves us,
what
we dream
and hope for.
We, wanderers
among the remote stars!

59 SPACES

There are places where
the soul rests.
There are voids where
the mind is quiet.
There are proximities
where the heart beats.

Internal spaces
intimately ours,
empty spaces
silently ours,
spaces where that moment,
full of infinity,

becomes knowledge
of oneself,
of the other,
becomes love,
becomes prayer,
becomes a gift.

60 BURNING STARS

Burning stars
in this clear
and infinite sky.
A cold
and sparkling
winter night.

You burn in my chest,
while my gaze
searches for a sign
that is not silent to my heart
and does not deny knowledge
to my thirst for insight.

Happiness without words,
eyes shining with tears.
Clenched fists
on my chest
while my brow
bends like the sky.

Empty and full of infinity,
immersed in mystery,
a creature that in trust
opens,
trying to live
among these overwhelming stars.

61 ILLUMINATION

As the river flows
to the sea,
so truths flow
into man.

62 TRUTH

Doubt
is atrocious,
but it forges
the soul.

63 SIGH

This year the summer
is not hot.

Perhaps man doesn't
deserve you, sun!

Sun! Does man no longer
know how to love?

Love is life and warmth,
and the new shoots
want to give.

I believe, sun, that
you will return to warm us!

64 I HEAR SINGING

I hear singing inside
a hymn to courage,
a song to faith.
I live among caged souls
and heads bowed to the
will of a reality
that is not true,
and is not false.

It is thus, as it appears
in the mirror
of the mind that
refracts
the images
of the theater of life.
Tomorrow will be,
beyond is hope!

65 MY HEART

My heart
longs for stars.

PRAYERS

66 PRAYER

Prayer
is the loving
friend of the heart
throughout the adventure
of our lives.

In prayer,
I rest myself in
God's hands.

67 OH GREAT LIGHT!

Oh great light
of love,
Oh joy of our
hearts,
Oh infinite good
for all,
Thy will be done.

68 FEAR NOT, MY SOUL!

Fear not, my soul!
High and clear the light will become.
New steps will find their way
to the rock
where one can rest
before falling upon the end
of the Mystery.

. . . and let the new adventure be
in the Infinite Love of God.

69 THE LITTLE LIGHT

There is a burning in my chest,
an emptiness to be filled
with an act
of love.

A little light
kindles in me
that breath,
that sigh that,
inside, wells up
as a disturbance,
and tomorrow comes
as deep song.
It becomes a human song.

Oh, God
my God of love,
how many times have I seen
my soul battered by torment
or in stasis,
but You, always,
are sweet to me,
you are the honey and
force of life!

70 THANK YOU IS A POOR EXPRESSION

The branch
of the pruned bush vibrates.
A tremor, which a strong
tension, wants to express
a thank you to heaven that,
slowly, opens into spring.

I feel within me this aspiration
of the earth, and everything speaks
of the harmony and unity of creation.

I pray, to feel part
of this orchestrated song,
like a flower, like a tree,
like a stone, like a cloud or a leaf.

To exist in unity
and in the Mystery that sings
Praise the Lord.

Thank you is a poor expression
to tell You what I feel!
Only silence,
calm and deep,
widens a circle within me
that radiates love,
expanding love.

71 A MOTHER'S PRAYERS

I surprised my mother
this morning, while she was praying.
Lying in her bed,
her lids lowered,
one hand on her forehead
and one on her chin, she was praying.
Her white hair was disheveled,
a diaphanous halo around her,
in the dimly lit room.

Her words,
like dewdrops,
were whispered in the
morning prayer,
softly, from her heart
to her lips,
in an imperceptible sound,
which was the echo of her
abandoned soul.

72 GUARDIAN ANGEL

Light of service and love,
voice of support and guidance,
Our Angel, we always
feel you beside us.

You welcomed us between your wings
from our first breath,
leaving the still warm womb
of our mother.

Together until the final ascent
when our soul,
freed and strengthened, will return
to the universal energy.

New visions in flight
will give us answers
that in life had no words,
always with you we will not be alone.

Our souls will lay by
the harvest of life and
conscious, purified,
clothed with love, in that eternal moment,
flooded with joy and wonder
they will contemplate the enchantment
of Your holy face.

73 AS GOD WILLS

Love will wash away all pain,
compassion will overturn weakness,
action will suck up all energy,
work will teach us the rhythms
of life.

Knowledge will calm anguish,
trust will dissolve fear,
deep friendship will defeat loneliness.

Children will patiently love
their parents,
parents will lovingly guide
their children to independence.

The order of good will fill
the void of evil,
and then everything will be
as God wills.

74 BITTER TEARS

Bitter and disappointed tears
for what holds me back
and hinders my becoming,
atrocious resistance,
those revels
deep within me.

Every hope
seems to shatter
like a wave
on the hard gray
rocks.

My God . . .
I feel like earth,
I feel like fire,
I feel like water,
but I wish I were air,
to be closer to you.

75 STRONG IN ME

Be strong in me
faith
that a new time will come,
a new world
of new stars
to look to.

76 TO FEDERICA

Little Angel,
watching the stars
you were snatched away.

Little Angel,
you lived an instant
and went back to the sky.

We did not ever rock you
or embrace you,
but we know you
in your father's and mother's love,
we know you
as the perfume in their lives.

This pain is too much, too
heavy and overflowing
only silence can help,
only prayer can
contemplate it.

Father help us to accept
this inconsolable Mystery.
Father, sustain who ever suffers,
hold out your hands.

77 THANK YOU

Thank you, my God
for giving me the strength to love!

78 INVOCATION

Great and merciful Lord,
within me
the flames are
blazing.

An energy I cannot
interpret,
a suffering that is not
open to knowledge,
a torment that
closes my throat,
hardens my actions,
disrupts every thought
and takes away my resolve.

Great Father,
in what can I serve you?
To what can I give myself
and thus give rest
to my mind?
I am slowly dying
within myself.

79 LORD

Lord,
in You alone is there
refreshment for a heart
aspiring to a
change
that struggles to come.

80 HEIMDALL'S HORN

Tell me, shepherd,
why do you call me?
I have heard your horn blowing:
Here I am!
I am with those who have harmony in their hearts.
I have no merit, for only duty lives in me,
called by a God
who loves the universe.

Tell me, shepherd,
what must I do?
Not yet knowing the place
where to act,
I have lived in darkness,
in silence, but now my wings
tickle me
to fly.

Tell me, shepherd,
who are my companions?
I want to be able to love them
and walk safely with them,
even if all around
darkness divides,
fear triumphs,
action stalls
and anguish rises.

Tell me, shepherd,
what means should I use?
I do not know the places
where I can walk.

Thank you, shepherd!
Thank you,
for waking me up
and reorienting me
to living well.

81 THE DAY OF THE EPIPHANY

And I, Lord,
thought you
had abandoned me,
the earth within me was boiling,
yet lifeless,
without heat.

You, suddenly,
like a comet,
reappeared,
illuminating the symbols
of your love
for me.

Epiphany, it is the day
and I adore you!

82 BEING PRESENT

Being present,
continuing,
uphill against the cold wind
that sweeps away dreams;
believing in the value
we carry in our hearts,
being faithful to the pact
of love that binds us to God,
certain that His Grace
will assist us.

The new time will discover us alive!

83 IN MY PRESENT

My present
has a new flavor:
awareness and love.

In my present
I enjoy civilization,
my country, and my language.

In my present
I love my family,
children and grandchildren.

In my present
I offer my services
and skills in my job.

In my present
I get pleasure from
my social life and people I meet.

In my present
I live and vibrate
the spirit of art.

In my present
I serve, obedient,
my destiny.

In my present
every instant
I yearn for God.

In my present
I welcome everything
with a smile.

In my present
towards a new path,
I am ready!

84 STABLE HEART

My heart is stable
at this moment . . .
and I rock gently
in the feeling that
floods me internally.
It is a thank you, for
this feeling of calm.
Serene, present, collected.

My heart is filled
with this feeling
deep within myself,
in thoughts of love,
of gratitude,
of awareness.
Thank you, my God, for this
gift of contemplation.

85 YOUR ARMS, LORD

Your arms, Lord,
open over us
like two great wings,
and with you, for a moment,
we arch out toward the infinite
love you have given us.

Your illuminated crucifix
is hope, the final point
beyond which, for us,
an uncontainable darkness opens up.

You, there, eternal,
speak to those who seek you.
You speak to those who escape you,
you speak to those who forget you.
You, in that corner of the church,
are peace, calm, strength, guidance!

AFTERWORD

By Don Alessio Romano, molto reverendo, former parish priest of St. Grata inter vites—Bergamo Alta, Italy.

A Tribute to *Epiphany of Light* and Luisella Traversi Guerra, upon twenty-three years of ministry.

Over the years, I have come to know and appreciate Luisella Traversi Guerra's multifaceted talent by observing how she practices her Christian dimension with such great dedication. I use the term "multifaceted" because within Luisella many human aspects vividly coexist. There is the woman, the wife, the mother, the educator, the corporate and cultural figure, then the philanthropist, poet, artist, author, and of course, the believer with a profound faith, from which she draws light and strength for her journey. In Luisella seven human dimensions are present, which I would describe as electromagnetic waves, that can be perceived and experienced just as the seven colors of the rainbow each contribute to the beauty and mystery of universal light.

I confess my own intellectual limitations when faced with such complex and elevated verses. However, I have accepted this task of writing about the collection, both in gratitude for the testimony of life they represent and as a way of thanking Luisella for her constant participation in the Church, especially in the Eucharistic celebrations, where she often serves as lector of the Sacred Scriptures.

1. Luisella the woman can be met in her poetry, her strong and tenacious attachment to life emerges clearly in words such as "Good morning, Life, so demanding, so impenetrable in the mystery that surrounds you; but life, life, life that lives in me!"

2. Wife and now widow, she offers her reflections on relationships in works like *We looked at each other smiling* and *Husband and Wife.*

3. A devoted mother of five and grandmother of nine, she lovingly raised her family, and dedicates numerous verses to dealing with children, growth, development and its challenges—which naturally leads to the next aspect.

4. Luisella the Educator, where her role extends beyond the family, touching didactics, culture, and above all guiding values. Her poem *Amongst the Ancestors* recites "How I wish to be a flash of light, in the present of my life! To finally rest without fear of having sown evil, falsehood, or weakness. I want to live with nobility and dignity. I aspire to do good."

5. As an author and poet, she has published dozens of works over the decades. A cascade of thoughts, feelings, and reflections emerges from her words. *Christmas is Coming, Winter Morning, My Garden* and *Silence in my Home* are examples of this. Her poems show deep emotion and sensitivity, anchored in everyday life yet open to the transcendent.

6. She is a prolific international artist, and her artistic eye transforms nature into vibrant emotion. In *February Morning* she writes "I gaze at the enchantment of the Sun splitting the rainy gray of winter, inside a pink cloud—how serene is my heart! Good day, life!". Also, in *Places of the World* we read "From meadows to cities, rivers to oceans, and—most of all—the hidden places of the soul: Your world is there.

7. The seventh aspect is Luisella as a believer, the foundational characteristic that gives meaning to all the rest. There are very many examples in the fourth and final section of the collection called Prayers: *The Prayer, Oh Great Light* (Final verse: "Thy will be done."), *Easter* as well as *In My Present*—a poem where there is the flavor of my civilization, of my place, of my language.

The seven aspects converge in expressions of love for family and children, in the offering of service and work, in the joy of social life and people, and in the vibrancy of the spirit of art. We see how to act as an obedient servant of destiny, hungry for God in every moment, who welcomes everything with a smile, with the optimistic credo 'I am ready for a new journey." In conclusion, thank you, Luisella, for your rich and multifaceted testimony of life, expressed through such beautiful poems and prayers. Thank you for these flashes of light, colors, sounds, silences, and feelings that open minds and hearts, as we all walk together toward that place where eternal light shines. Let us hold onto the consoling Gospel verse from Matthew 13:43, where Jesus promises:

"Then the righteous will shine like the sun in the kingdom of their Father. Whoever has ears, let them hear."

Our search for light will be fulfilled in its totality in the encounter with the Father.

Don Allessio Romano
October 12, 2025

ACKNOWLEDGMENTS

In gratitude to all those who have helped bring this new collection of poems and prayers to light, I wish that it will sustain and support every reader who discovers it, guiding each on their own individual path to upliftment.

Luisella Traversi Guerra

Editing and translating Luisella Traversi Guerra's incredibly vast patrimony of poems and prayers was a delightfully labyrinthine challenge, after which I can confirm that her works are intensely transformative and redemptive of even the most thoroughly lost souls. *Epiphany of Light* is a particularly unique collection because it unites many of her past works with hitherto unpublished spiritual verses, borrowing a noble aim from her beloved Harmonists—that of inspiring her audience towards the pursuit of betterment through her constant and lifelong motto and mantra—I aspire to do good.

The Third movement, Verses for America, draws from the poet's charitable work with Boy's Town of Omaha, and her many happy years in Evansville, Indiana, where she also set her 2024 work of Christian fiction, *The Story of Lucy Belmont*.

Special thanks to Matt, Hannah, Calvin and Shannon for their careful reading and creative input during the publishing process.

Margaret Louise Fitzgibbon

BIOGRAPHY

Luisella Traversi Guerra is a well-known Italian poet, author and painter. She has published five volumes of poetry as well as many children's books, fiction for youths and adults, and works of motivational and manegerial non-fiction. She is also an affirmed oil painter who exhibits all around the globe. In 2024 she released *The Story of Lucy Belmont*, a lyrical work of Christian fiction set in her beloved Evansville, Indiana. *Epiphany of Light* is a selection of her past and present spiritual verses and prayers.

Born on July 21st, 1944 in Borgonovo (Piacenza, Italy) she spent her childhood in Paris and then returned to Italy in the early 1950s. She married in 1963 and has five children, as well as nine grandchildren. For more on her writing and activities, and to enroll for her quarterly newsletter, visit www.luisellatraversiguerra.com. For more on her painting visit www.ltgatelier.com.

www.ingramcontent.com/pod-product-compliance
Lightning Source LLC
LaVergne TN
LVHW051132080426
835510LV00018B/2372